# Practical Guide to the Operational Use of the FN FAL Rifle

By Erik Lawrence

Copyright© 2017 Erik Lawrence

All rights reserved. No part of this book may be reproduced or transmitted in any form or by any means, electronic or mechanical, including photocopying, recording, or by an information storage and retrieval system, without permission in writing from the publisher. Exceptions to this include reviewers who may quote brief passages in a review to be printed in a magazine, newspaper, or on the Internet. For information, please contact

Erik Lawrence
www.vig-sec.com    erik@vig-sec.com

Although the author and publisher have made every effort to ensure the accuracy and completeness of information contained in this book, we assume no responsibility for the use or misuse of information contained in this book and errors, inaccuracies, omissions, or any inconsistency herein. Portions of this manual are excerpts from outside sources but been validated and modified as necessary.

**Printed and bound in the United States of America**

**First printing 2017**

**ISBN: 978-1-961989-10-8**
eBook ISBN: 978-1-961989-12-2

ATTENTION U.S. MILITARY UNITS, U.S. GOVERNMENT AGENCIES, AND PROFESSIONAL ORGANIZATIONS: Quantity discounts are available on bulk purchases of this book. Special books or book excerpts can also be created to fit specific needs. For information, please contact

Erik Lawrence
www.vig-sec.com    erik@vig-sec.com

Firearms are potentially dangerous and must be handled responsibly by individuals. The technical information presented in this manual on the use of the FN FAL reflects the author's research, beliefs, and experiences. The information in this book is presented for academic study only. Neither the author nor the publisher assumes any responsibility for the use or misuse of information contained in this book.

SAFETY NOTICE
Before starting an inspection, ensure the weapon is cleared. Do not manipulate the trigger until the weapon has been cleared of all ammunition. Inspect the chamber to ensure that it is empty and no ammunition is present. Keep the weapon oriented in a safe direction when loading and handling.

AMMUNITION NOTICE- Firing the incorrect ammunition will damage the weapon and possibly injure the operator.

Training should be received from knowledgeable and experienced operators on this weapons system. Vigilant Security Services, LLC® provides this training and continually perfects its instruction with up-to-date information from actual use.

www.vig-sec.com

# Table of Contents

## Section 1 ................................................................................. 1
### Introduction ............................................................................ 1
#### Description ........................................................................... 2
#### Background ........................................................................... 3
#### Variants ............................................................................. 6

## Section 2 ................................................................................ 12
### Nomenclature .......................................................................... 12
#### Maintenance .......................................................................... 12
### Clearing the FAL Rifle ................................................................ 14
#### Disassembling the FAL Rifle ......................................................... 16
#### Cleaning the FAL Rifle .............................................................. 21
#### Reassembling the FAL Rifle ......................................................... 24
#### Performing a Function Check on the FAL Rifle ....................................... 27

## Section 3 ................................................................................ 29
### Operation and Function ................................................................ 29
#### Loading the FAL ..................................................................... 32
#### Firing positions for the FAL Rifle .................................................. 39
#### Firing the FAL Rifle ................................................................ 40
#### Launching Grenades with the FAL Rifle .............................................. 41

## Section 4 ................................................................................ 43
### Performance Problems .................................................................. 43
#### Malfunction and Immediate Action Procedures ........................................ 43

# Section 1

## Introduction

The objective of this manual is to allow the reader to be able to use the FN FAL competently. The manual will give the reader background/specifications of the weapon; instruct on its operation, disassembly, and assembly; detail proper firing procedure; and identify malfunction/misfire procedures. Operator-level maintenance will also be detailed to allow the reader to understand fully and become competent in the use and maintenance of the FN FAL rifle.

**Figure 1-1 FN FAL**

## Description

The FN FAL or Light Automatic Rifle is a gas-regulated piston automatic weapon, caliber 7.62x51mm NATO, gas-operated and with a tilting breech block, which is mechanically locked before firing can take place. In the short-stroke piston system (tappet system) - the piston moves separately from the bolt group. It may directly push the bolt group parts as in the M1 carbine or operate through a connecting rod.

The characteristics of the FN FAL Rifle

**Figure 1-2 FN FAL**

A. Country of Origin: Belgium

B. Military Designation: FN FAL

C. Operation: Full and semi-automatic fire

D. Cartridge: 7.62x51mm (.308 Winchester)

E. Ammunition: All standard NATO and commercial loads

F. Length: 43 inches (1,090mm)

G. Barrel: 21 inches (533mm), right-hand twist

H. Weight (unloaded): 9.5 lb. (4.3kg)

I. Type of Feed: 20-round detachable box

J. Operating System: Gas-operated, tilting breechblock

K. Rate of Fire: 700 rpm

L. Muzzle Velocity: 2,750 fps (840 m/s)

M. Maximum Effective Range: 600 meters

N. Sights: Aperture rear sight with a post front sight. The sight radius is 21 inches (553mm).

## Background

In 1946, the first FN FAL prototype was completed. It was designed to fire the intermediate 7.92x33mm Kurz cartridge developed and used by the forces of Nazi Germany during World War II (see StG44 assault rifle). After testing this prototype in 1948, the British Army urged FN to build additional prototypes, including one in bullpup configuration, chambered for their new .280 British caliber intermediate cartridge. After evaluating the single bullpup prototype, FN decided to return instead to its original, conventional design for future production.

In 1950, the United Kingdom presented the redesigned FN rifle and the British EM-2, both in .280 British caliber, to the United States for comparison testing against the favored United States Army design of the time -- Earle Harvey's T25. It was hoped that a common cartridge and rifle could be standardized for issue to the armies of all NATO member countries. After this testing was completed, U.S. Army officials suggested that FN should redesign its rifle to fire the U.S. prototype ".30 Light Rifle" cartridge. FN decided to hedge its bets with the U.S., and in 1951 even made a deal that the U.S. could produce FALs royalty-free, given that the UK appeared to be favoring their own EM-2.

This decision appeared to be correct when the British Army decided to adopt the EM-2 and .280 British cartridge in the very same month – a decision This decision was later rescinded after the Labor Party lost the 1951 General Election and Winston Churchill returned as Prime Minister. The .30 Light Rifle cartridge was in fact later standardized as the 7.62 mm NATO; however, the U.S. insisted on continued rifle tests. The FAL chambered for the .30 Light Rifle went up against the redesigned T25 (now redesignated as the T47) and an M1 Garand variant, the T44. Eventually, the T44 won, becoming the M14. However, in the meantime, most other NATO countries were evaluating and selecting the FAL.

The FAL, or *Fusil Automatique Léger* ("Light Automatic Rifle" or L.A.R.), is a semi-automatic/selective fire battle rifle produced by the Belgian armaments manufacturer Fabrique Nationale de Herstal (FN) from 1953 to the present day. The rifle was developed from 1947 until 1953, and the designers were Dieudonne Saive and Ernest Vervier of FN. During the Cold War, it was adopted by many North Atlantic Treaty Organization (NATO) countries, with the notable exception of the United States. It is one of the most widely used rifles in history, having been used by more than 90 countries. There are 2,000,000 -- plus rifles manufactured by numerous different factories around the world. IMBEL is an acronym for Indústria de Material Bélico do Brasil (War Material Industry of Brazil) a Brazilian state company, founded in 1975 as a quango of the Ministry of Defence, which also made many of the world's FNs.

The FAL was predominantly chambered for the 7.62x51mm NATO round (although originally designed for the .280 British intermediate cartridge), and because of its prevalence and widespread use among the armed forces of many NATO countries during the Cold War, it was nicknamed "The right arm of the Free World." A British Commonwealth derivative of the FN FAL has been produced under license as the L1A1 Self-Loading Rifle. The British model is an inch-patterned receiver and not metric like the others.

**FN production variants**

LAR 50.41 & 50.42
Also known as FALO as an abbreviation from the French *Fusil Automatique Lourd*; heavy barrel for sustained fire with 30-round magazine as a squad automatic weapon. Known in Canada as the C2A1, it was their primary squad automatic weapon until it was phased out during the 1980s in favor of the C9, which has better accuracy and higher ammunition capacity than the C2. Known to the Australian Army as the L2A1, it was replaced by the FN Minimi. The L2A1 or "heavy barrel" FAL was used by several Commonwealth nations and was found to experience frequently a failure to feed after firing two rounds from a full magazine when in automatic mode. The 50.41 is fitted with a synthetic buttstock, while the 50.42's buttstock is made from wood.

FAL 50.61
Folding stock, standard length barrel paratrooper model with folding charging handle, Figure 1-3.

**Figure 1-3 FAL 50.61 variant with a folding stock and standard barrel length**

FAL 50.62
Folding-stock, shorter 17" (458mm) barrel, paratrooper version with folding charging handle.

FAL 50.63
Folding-stock, shorter 17" (436mm) barrel, paratrooper version with folding charging handle. This shorter version was requested by Belgian paratroopers. The upper receiver was not cut for a carry handle; the bolt stop device was absent, which allowed the folded-stock rifle to fit through the doorway of their C-119 Flying Boxcar when worn horizontally across the chest.

FAL 50.64
Folding stock, standard barrel length, "Hiduminium" aluminum alloy lower receiver. The charging handle on the 50.64 was a folding model like the L1A1 rifles.

FAL OSW (DSA-58 OSW - Operational Special Weapon)
Folding stock, shorter 13" (330mm) barrel, paratrooper version.

## Variants

## L1A1 – England

**Figure 1-4 L1A1 wood stock**

**Figure 1-5 L1A1 plastic stock**

**Caliber:** 7.62x51mm NATO

**Type:** Short-stroke piston system (tappet system), gas-operated, tilting breechblock

**Overall length:** 45 inches (1,143mm)

**Weight unloaded:** 9.5 lb. (4.3kg)

**Barrel length:** 21 inches (554mm)

**Magazine capacity:** 20, detachable box magazine

**Rate of Fire**: 650-750 rounds per minute (rpm)

**Maximum Effective Range**: 800 meters

The L1A1 Self-Loading Rifle is also known as the SLR, by the Canadian Army designation C1A1 (C1), or in the USA as the "inch pattern" FAL. It is a British Commonwealth derivative of the Belgian FN FAL battle rifle *(Fusil Automatique Léger* ["Light Automatic Rifle"] produced by the Belgian armaments manufacturer Fabrique Nationale de Herstal [FN]). The L1A1 is produced under license and has seen use in the Australian Army, Canadian Army, Indian Army, Jamaica

Defence Force, Malaysian Army, New Zealand Army, Rhodesian Army, South African Defence Force, and the British Armed Forces.

The original FAL was designed in Belgium using metric dimensions, while the components of the "inch-pattern" FALs are manufactured to a slightly modified design using British imperial units. Many sub-assemblies are interchangeable between the two types, while components of those sub-assemblies may not be compatible. Notable incompatibilities include the magazines and the butt-stock, which attach in different ways.

Most Commonwealth pattern FALs are semi-automatic only. A variant named L2A1/C2A1 (C2), meant to serve as a light machine gun in a support role, is also capable of automatic fire. Differences from the L1A1/C1 include a heavy barrel, squared front sight (versus the "V" on the semi-automatic models), a handguard that doubles as a foldable bipod, and a larger 30-round magazine, although it could also use the normal 20-round magazines. Only Australia and Canada used this variant, as the UK and New Zealand used Bren light machine guns converted to fire the 7.62x51mm NATO cartridge. Canadian C1s issued to naval and army personnel were also capable of automatic fire.

## IMBEL - Brazil

**Figure 1-6 IMBEL FAL**

**Caliber:** 7.62x51mm NATO

**Type:** Short-stroke piston system (tappet system), gas-operated, tilting breechblock

**Overall length:** Varies depending on the model

**Weight unloaded:** Varies depending on the model

**Barrel length:** Varies depending on the model

**Magazine capacity:** 20, detachable box magazine

**Rate of Fire**: 700 rounds per minute (rpm)

**Maximum Effective Range**: 800 meters

- IMBEL offers the FAL in 9 versions:
- M964, the standard-length barrel, semi-auto and full auto
- M964 MD1, short barrel, semi-auto and full auto
- M964 MD2, standard length barrel, semi-auto only
- M964 MD3, short barrel, semi-auto only
- M964A1, folding stock standard barrel, semi-auto and full auto
- M964A1 MD1, folding stock short barrel, semi-auto and full auto
- M964A1 MD2, folding stock standard barrel, semi-auto only
- M964A1 MD3, folding stock short barrel, semi-auto only
- M964A1, short barrel, semi-auto and full auto with Picatinny rail

## FAL V (FAL M5) – Argentina

Figure 1-7 FAL V

**Caliber:** 7.62x51mm NATO

**Type:** Short-stroke piston system (tappet system), gas-operated, tilting breechblock

**Overall length:** Varies depending on the model

**Weight unloaded:** Varies depending on the model

**Barrel length:** Varies depending on the model

**Magazine capacity:** 20, detachable box magazine

**Rate of Fire:** 700 rounds per minute (rpm)

**Maximum Effective Range:** 800 meters

- **FAMTD**: *Fusil Argentino Modelo Tirador Destacado - Cañón Pesado* (Argentine Designated Marksman Rifle - Heavy Barrel). Designated Marksman Rifle (DMR) variant. It has a range of 650 meters.
- **FAMTD**: *Fusil Argentino Modelo Tirador Destacado - Cañón Liviano* (Argentine Designated Marksman Rifle - Light Barrel). It has a light bipod and a telescopic sight (10 × 50) with mounting for night vision.
- **FAMA**: *Fusil Argentino Modelo Asalto* (Argentine Assault Rifle Model). This is the assault rifle version, using 7.62 ammunition. It has a rate of 700 rounds per minute, and it has a length of 591 mm. Able to incorporate holographic view, laser flashlight, tactical grip, or a 40mm grenade launcher.
- **FAMCa**: *Fusil Argentino Modelo Carabina* (Argentine Rifle Carbine Model). This is the carbine variant.

# FAL – Israel

**Figure 1-8 Israeli FAL Heavy Barrel**

**Caliber:** 7.62x51mm NATO

**Type:** Short-stroke piston system (tappet system) gas-operated, tilting breechblock

**Overall length:** Varies depending on the model

**Weight unloaded:** Varies depending on the model

**Barrel length:** Varies depending on the model

**Magazine capacity:** 20, detachable box magazine

**Rate of Fire:** 700 rounds per minute (rpm)

**Maximum Effective Range:** 800 meters

The IDF decided to adopt the FN FAL as its standard-issue infantry rifle, under the name *Rov've Mitta'enn* or *Romat* (רו"מט), an abbreviation of "Self-loading Rifle." The FAL version ordered by the IDF came in two basic variants, both regular and heavy-barrel (automatic rifle), and were chambered for 7.62mm NATO ammunition. In common with heavy-barrel FALs used by several other nations, the Israeli "heavy barrel" FAL (called the *Makle'a Kal*, or *Makleon*) was found to experience frequently a failure to feed after firing two rounds from a full magazine when in automatic mode. The Israeli FALs were originally produced as selective-fire rifles, though later light-barrel rifle versions were altered to semi-automatic fire only. The Israeli models are recognizable by a distinctive handguard with a forward perforated sheet metal section, a rear wood section unlike most other FALs in shape, and their higher "Commonwealth"-type sights.

## STG 58 Strumgewehr 58 – Austria

**Figure 1-9 STG 58**

**Caliber:** 7.62x51mm NATO

**Type:** Short-stroke piston system (tappet system), gas-operated, tilting breechblock

**Overall length:** 43 inches (1,090mm)

**Weight unloaded:** 9.5 lb. (4.3kg)

**Barrel length:** 21 inches (533mm), right-hand twist

**Magazine capacity:** 20, detachable box magazine

**Rate of Fire:** 700 rounds per minute (rpm)

**Maximum Effective Range:** 800 meters

The STG 58 was built by Steyr under license from FN and incorporated the flash hider, grenade launcher, barbed wire cutter, and the L-shaped gas plug release lever. They were modeled off the German G1 FAL variants and used the metal handguards.

# Section 2

## Nomenclature

## Maintenance

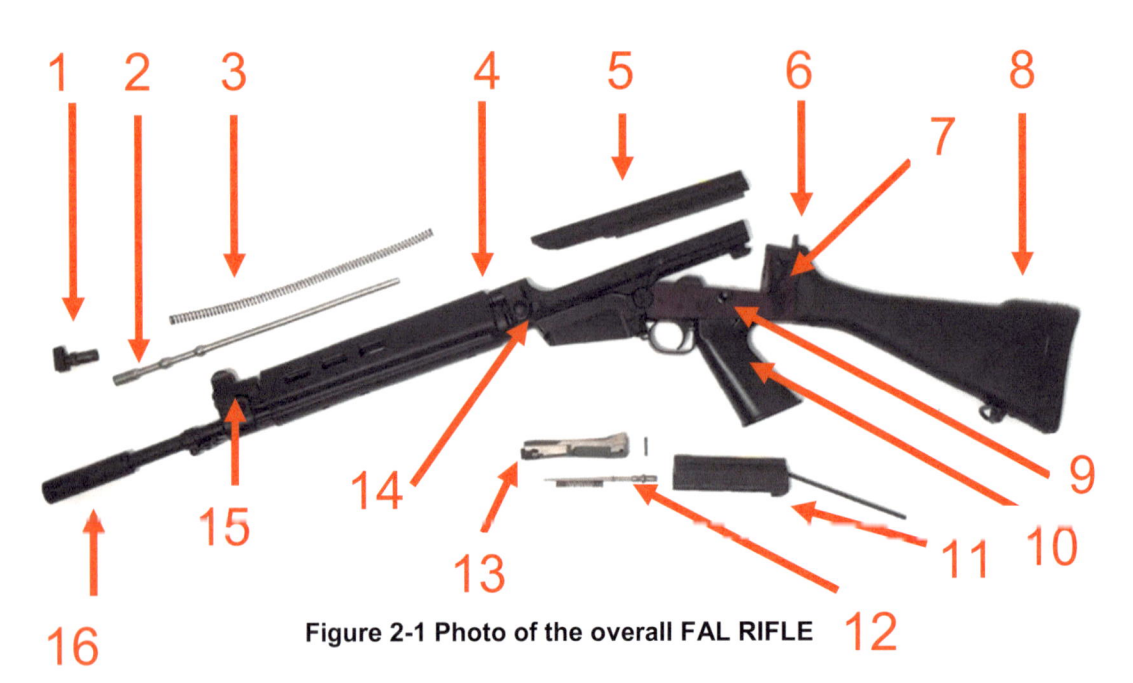

Figure 2-1 Photo of the overall FAL RIFLE

1- Gas Plug
2- Piston Rod
3- Piston Spring
4- Upper Receiver Assembly
5- Receiver Cover
6- Rear Sight
7- Receiver Locking Lever
8- Buttstock
9- Selector Lever
10- Pistol Grip
11- Bolt Carrier
12- Firing Pin and Spring
13- Bolt
14- Charging Handle
15- Front Sight
16- Muzzle

Practical Guide to the Operational Use of the FN FAL Rifle

**Figure 2-2 Photo of the control parts of the FAL**

1- Charging Handle  2- Magazine Well  3- Bolt Hold Open Device
4- Magazine Release Lever  5- Trigger Guard  6- Trigger
7- Selector Lever  8- Receiver Locking Lever

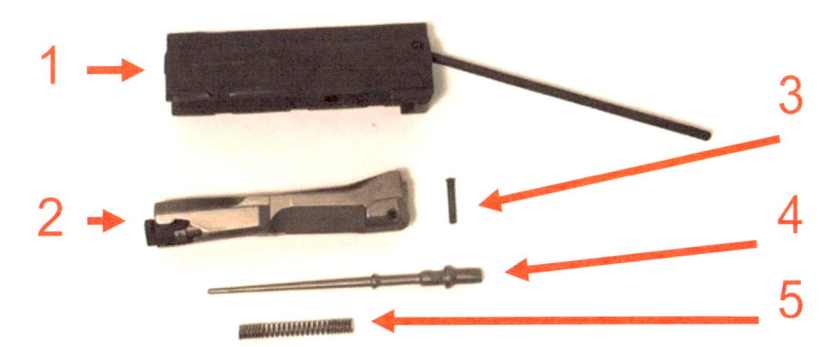

**Figure 2-3 Photo of the disassembled bolt assembly of the FAL**

1- Bolt Carrier  2- Bolt  3- Firing Pin Retaining Pin
4- Firing Pin  5- Firing Pin Spring

**NOTE**- Depending on the country and/or year of manufacture there are variations to the sights, bolt hold open/release, firing pins, gas tube orientation, gas plugs, and magazine release levers. Functionally they are the same but may be different from the original design. I will attempt to show variants where needed.

## Clearing the FAL Rifle

**Figure 2-4 FAL Selector Lever**

A. Ensure the rifle is on SAFE (S) (Figure 2-4) and pointed in a safe direction.

**Figure 2-5a**          **Figure 2-5b**

B. Remove the magazine by pressing the magazine catch forward (Figure 2-5a) and rotate the magazine from the magazine well (Figure 2-5b). Place the magazine in a pocket, magazine pouch or set it down.

**Figure 2-6a reverse grip**          **Figure 2-6b**

C. Pull the charging handle rearward with your left hand (palm down) (Figure 2-6a), allowing the round to extract and eject from the rifle.

Press up on the bolt hold open device and release the tension on the charging handle to lock the bolt to the rear (Figure 2-6b). Observe the round extracting and ejecting from the ejection port; do not attempt to retain the round.

**Figure 2-7**

D. Visually and physically check the chamber for rounds (Figure 2-7). Once you have ensured the rifle has no magazine in it and the chamber is free of rounds, you now can close the bolt by pulling the charging handle to the rear and riding the bolt forward so as not to forcefully shut on an empty chamber.

**Figure 2-8 Child soldier in Africa with FAL**

## Disassembling the FAL Rifle

NOTE- Place the rifle's parts on a flat, clean surface with the muzzle oriented in a safe direction. For this field stripping, the operator will need to use the nose of a cartridge; no other tools are required. Cock the mechanism to ensure that the rifle is clear and there is no round left in the chamber, allow the bolt carrier to go forward, and set the selector lever on SAFE, leaving the hammer cocked.

When the operator begins to disassemble the rifle, it should be done in the following order after it has been cleared as described previously:

**Figure 2-9a**     **Figure 2-9b**

A. With your right thumb, press the receiver locking lever (on the left side) to the rear (Figure 2-9b); at the same time, press the butt/rear of the rifle downwards, which will swing the rifle open like a shotgun (Figure 2-9b).

**Figure 2-10a**     **Figure 2-10b**

B. Pull out the bolt carrier assembly by grasping the bolt carrier hinged rod (Figure 2-10a) and then removing it from the receiver (Figure 2-10b). Lay down the bolt carrier assembly.

Figure 2-11a

Figure 2-11b

C. Slide the receiver cover to the rear (Figure 2-11a) and off (Figure 2-11b).

Figure 2-12a

Figure 2-12b

D. To separate the bolt carrier assembly, disengage the front part of the bolt from the bolt carrier (Figure 2-12a), and keeping and pressing the thumb on the rear of the firing pin to slightly compress the firing pin spring, continue to separate with a levering movement against the rear part of the bolt carrier (Figure 2-12b).

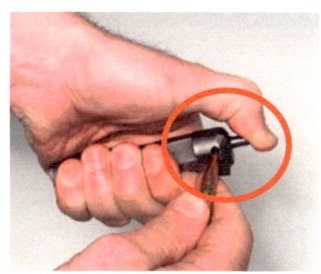

Figure 2-13a

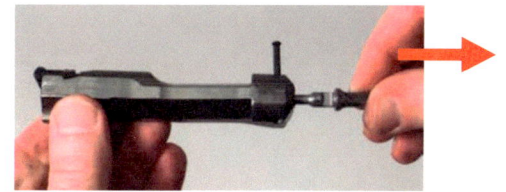

Figure 2-13b

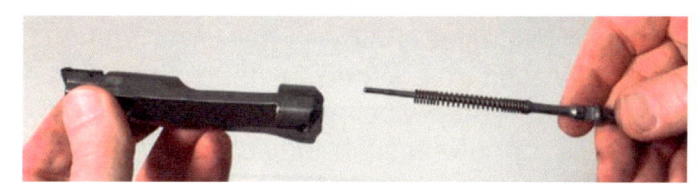

Figure 2-13c

E. To remove the firing pin, exert pressure on the rear end of the firing pin and push out its retaining pin. If the pin does not fall out easily, use the nose of a cartridge to push it out (Figure 2-13a). When the retaining pin has been removed, the firing pin will come out of its housing under action of its spring, then separate the firing pin spring from the firing pin (Figures 2-13b and 2-13c).

Figure 2-14a            Figure 2-14b

Figure 2-14c            Figure 2-14d

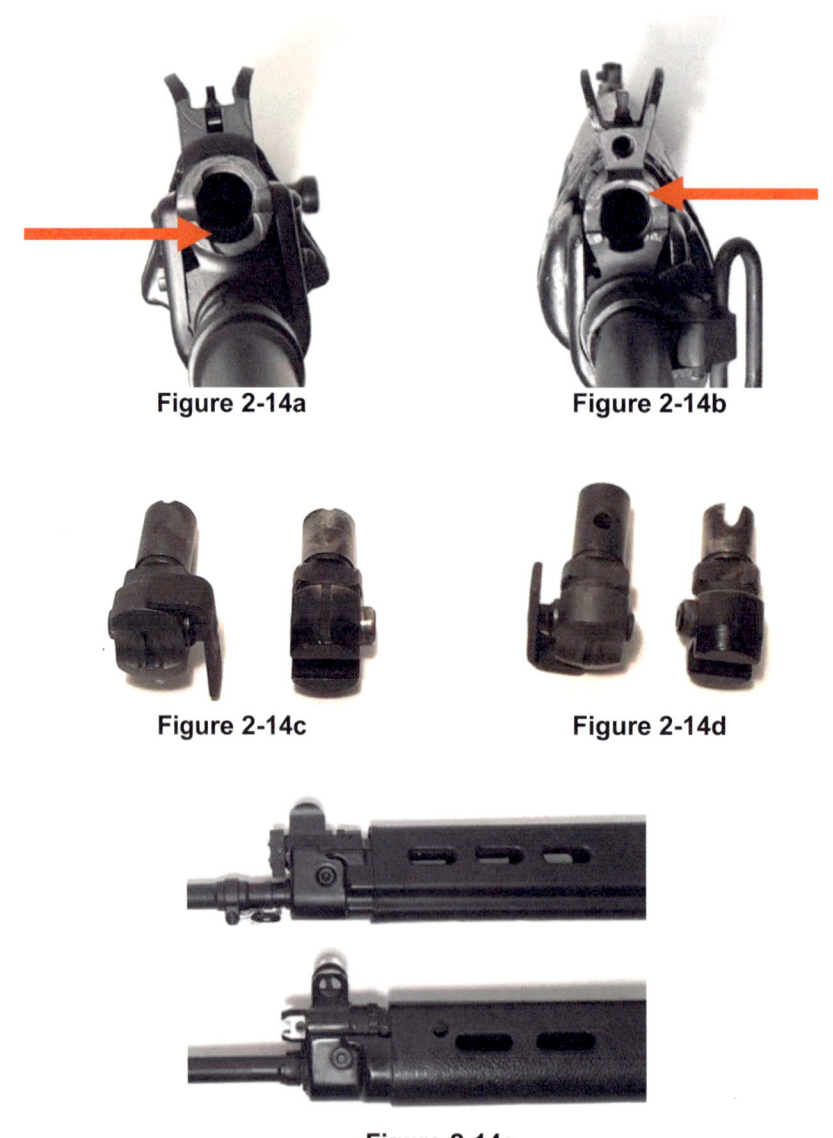

Figure 2-14e

Gas Plug Removal- There are several different types of gas plugs amongst the various models of FAL rifles. Below is the L1A1 and STG58 types of gas blocks and removal procedures. When in doubt look at the end of the gas tube and determine where the wide and narrow lug go to fit it into the gas tube prior to rotating it for automatic or single shot grenade fire mode. Notice the wide recess on the STG58 it is at the bottom of the gas tube (Figure 2-14a) and on the L1A1 is at the top of the gas tube (Figure 2-14b). The STG58 gas plug is on the left and the L1A1 gas plug is on the right in Figures 2-14c and 2-14d. Figure 2-14c shows the up position for automatic rifle fire (gas will operate the rifle), and Figure 2-14d shows the up position to shoot single shot (gas will not operate the rifle). Figure 2-14e has the STG58 on the top and the L1A1 on the bottom to show their gas plugs in automatic fire. One will have to adjust to taking out and replacing the gas plug into which ever rifle you are using. Some gas plugs are marked with an "A" for automatic and a "G" for grenade to simplify this.

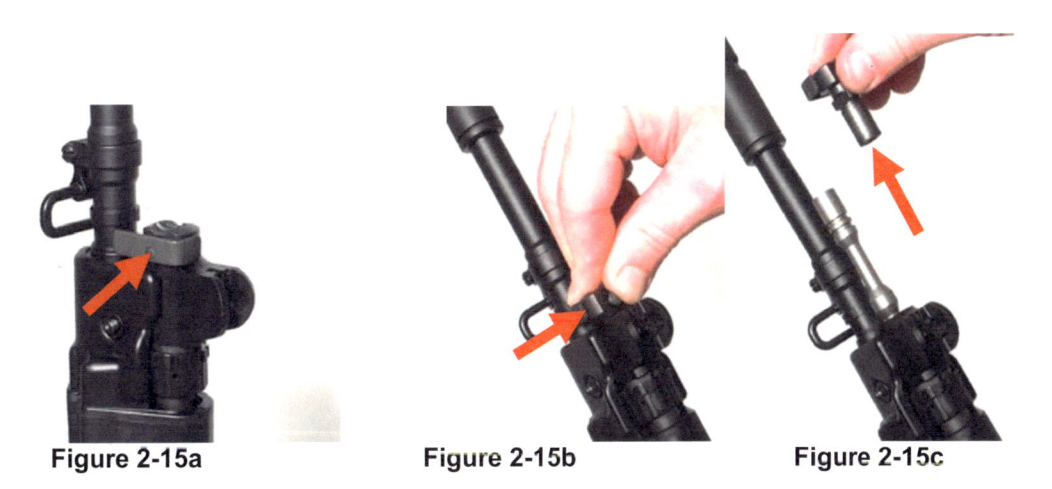

**Figure 2-15a**     **Figure 2-15b**     **Figure 2-15c**

F. STF58 Gas Plug Removal- To remove the gas plug, press in on the gas plug spring-loaded piece (knurled) (Figure 2-15a), and then turn the ==gas plug counter clockwise direction one complete turn (Figure 2-15b)==. In this position, the plug will be pushed from the gas tube by the piston spring (Figure 2-15c).

**Figure 2-16a**      **Figure 2-16b**      **Figure 2-16c**

L1A1 Gas Plug Removal- To remove the gas plug, press in on the gas plug spring-loaded piece with the tip of a cartridge (Figure 2-16a), and then turn the ==gas plug in a counterclockwise direction one complete turn (Figure 2-16b)==. In this position, the plug will be pushed from the gas tube by the piston spring (Figure 2-16c).

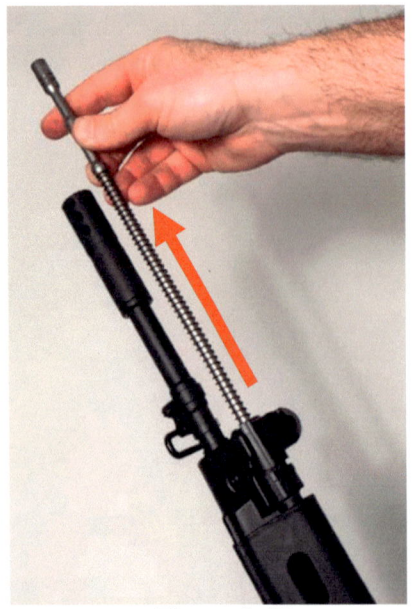

Practical Guide to the Operational Use of the FN FAL Rifle

**Figure 2-17a**  **Figure 2-17b**

G. Lift out the gas piston and spring (Figure 2-17a); remove the piston and its spring from the gas tube (Figure 2-17b).

**Figure 2-18**

H. Separate the piston spring from the piston rod (Figure 2-18).

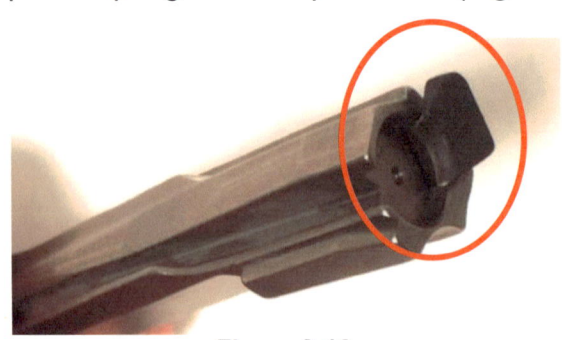

**Figure 2-19**

NOTE: There is no need for the shooter to strip the extractor (Figure 2-19). It is necessary to use a cartridge for this, or a special tool, and it is normally done by the armorer when making a periodic inspection.

## Cleaning the FAL Rifle

It must be emphasized that all automatic weapons require constant cleaning and maintenance and that most of the stoppages mentioned elsewhere are the result of the soldier's negligence or lack of knowledge of his weapon. All weapons, whether automatic or repeating rifles, should be cleaned at the end of a day's firing, and special care must be taken after firing with blank cartridges.

The barrel's bore and gas cylinder must be cleaned regularly so that they never get into such a state that the use of abrasives is necessary; all abrasive material, such as emery paper, sand, etc., is always harmful.

### Basic Cleaning and maintenance by the shooter

The FAL Rifle needs only to be stripped partially for this field maintenance (i.e., field stripping); maintenance routine is as follows:

Use the barrel cleaning brush, oiled with the powder solvent, and pass through the barrel several times. Follow this by pulling through two or three dry rags.
Clean the chamber with the cleaning brush provided for this purpose.

- Clean the bolt carrier, rear of the barrel and inside the body.
- Clean the bolt carrier, firing pin and its housing.
- Clean underneath the extractor claw, without stripping it;
- Remove the gas plug, the piston and its spring and carefully clean these parts, as they are exposed to gas fouling.
- Clean the gas cylinder and wipe with a slightly oiled rag; this rag should also be passed through the barrel.
- Very slightly oil the moving parts of the mechanism.

### Full Detailed Cleaning

The full cleaning of barrel and gas cylinder should be done unhurriedly, when circumstances permit, as follows:
- Clean the barrel using bore brush or swab with powder solvent on them.
- Clean the inside of the front part of the gas cylinder and gas block, using a brush for cleaning the chamber with the powder solvent.
- After the barrel and gas cylinder have been thoroughly cleaned in this way, dry carefully, using clean rags. After drying, the rag should come out of the barrel and gas cylinder unstained.
- After drying, slightly oil the barrel (bore and chamber) and the gas cylinder.
- Dry the outside of the barrel and wipe with a lightly oiled rag.

Change your tip out to a patch eyelet and patch so you may pass it through the bore; use an unfolded piece for cleaning the gas cylinder. Double patch it before inserting in the loop of the cleaning rod or pull-through-type bore snake.

Clean rags can be used for cleaning the remaining parts of the rifle.

Note: The inside of the barrel and the inside of front half of the gas cylinder come into direct contact with the combustion gases and are also submitted to friction; they consequently require more care and attention. Other components are protected against oxidizing by phosphating (parts of the mechanism and receiver), and the piston and gas plug are hard chromed.

**Precaution after Firing**

To be on the safe side, particularly in hot climates, and to make subsequent cleaning of barrel and gas cylinder easier, the user is strongly advised to take the following preventive measure:

Immediately after firing, before leaving the firing range, clean the barrel and gas cylinder by wiping with a rag and powder solvent.

This precaution has the effect of:
- Neutralizing the harmful effect of any fouling caused by residue of powder gases,
- Preventing the formation of carbon deposits in the gas cylinder and gas block,
- Allowing the usual cleaning operations to be postponed for at least 24 hours, without causing any damage.

Within 48 hours of carrying out this precaution, the rifle should be completely cleaned as indicated above.

**Preparation of the Rifle Prior to Firing**

The rifle functions with very little or practically no lubrication.

Before firing, wipe off any oil remaining on barrel and gas cylinder surfaces; if the piston and chromed part of the gas plug have been slightly oiled, dry clean these, too.

Components or parts of components which will be very slightly oiled
OILED
- Inside bolt carrier
- Bolt, to locking shoulders
- Body, at bottom and along guide grooves for bolt carrier
- Holding open device

Components or parts of components which will not be oiled before firing LEFT DRY
- Barrel
- Gas cylinder
- Piston chrome
- Gas plug and ports
- Outer surface of bolt carrier
- Front face of bolt carrier
- Magazine
- Magazine catch
- Sights

## Reassembling the FAL Rifle

A. Replace the piston spring onto the piston rod.

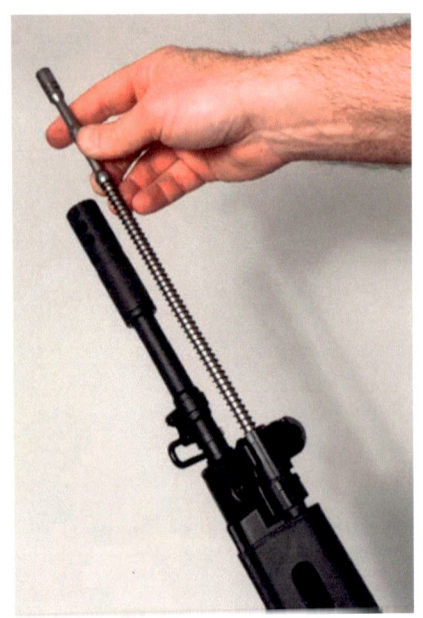

**Figure 2-20**

B. Replace the piston and its spring in the gas tube (Figure 2-20).

**Figure 2-21**

C. Determine where the wide lug is and the location on the gas tube of the wide recess as explained in the disassembly instructions and insert the gas plug. Press and hold down to compress the piston spring, and rotate it 1/8 of a turn to engage the lug that will hold it in the gas tube until the next step (Figure 2-21).

**Figure 2-22a**  **Figure 2-22b**

D. When the gas plug is fully inserted, rotate the gas plug clockwise so that the short leg of the L piece is on top (Figure 2-22a – STG58), the single cut groove is on top (Figure 2-22b - L1A1), or the letter "A" faces upwards if it is marked.

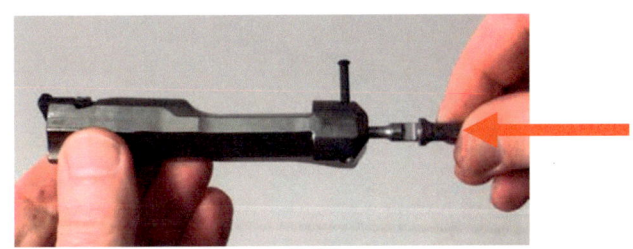

**Figure 2-22**

E. Start the firing pin retaining pin into its hole on the extractor side of the bolt and place the firing pin with its spring into the rear of the bolt (Figure 2-23); compress the spring by pressing the rear of the firing pin and push in the firing pin retaining pin until it is flush.

**Figure 2-24**

F. Replace the bolt in the bolt carrier, inserting the rear of the firing pin into the hole in the back of the bolt carrier (Figure 2-24). Exert pressure on the rear of the firing pin so that the firing pin spring is slightly compressed and the bolt is swung upwards into its correct position in the bolt carrier.

**Figure 2-25**

G. Insert the ribs of the cover into the corresponding grooves in the receiver (Figure 2-25) and slide the cover fully forward.

**Figure 2-26**

H. Replace the bolt carrier assembly in the receiver, inserting the rails of the bolt carrier in the corresponding grooves in the receiver. When this step is done, the bolt carrier should be in its forward position (Figure 2-26) and the muzzle of the rifle pointing downwards; the bolt carrier assembly will then fall into position correctly.

**Figure 2-27**

I. Close the rifle (Figure 2-27), holding the muzzle downwards to prevent any possibility of the bolt carrier rod protruding.

## Performing a Function Check on the FAL Rifle

### Safety and Function Check (Semi-Automatic only rifle)

- Ensure the weapon is clear of all ammunition.
- Pull charging handle to rear and release it. Place selector on SAFE (S). Squeeze the trigger, and the hammer should not fall.
- Place the selector on FIRE (R). Squeeze the trigger and hold the trigger to the rear. The hammer should fall. While holding the trigger to the rear, pull the charging handle to the rear and release it. Release the trigger, and you should hear a click as you release the trigger. Squeeze the trigger again; the hammer should fall.
- Pull charging handle to rear again, release, and then place the weapon on SAFE.

### Function Check Procedures (Semi- and Full-Automatic Rifle):

- Pull the charging handle to the rear and return it to its forward position.
- Place the weapon on SAFE.
- Pull the trigger; nothing should happen.
- Place the weapon on the SEMI - semi-automatic selector position.
- Pull the trigger, and the hammer should release; hold the trigger back.
- Pull the charging handle to the rear and release; let up on the trigger (hear the reset) and press the trigger to release the hammer (hear the hammer be released).
- Pull the charging handle to the rear and release, and place the weapon on the AUTO (A) - automatic-selector position.
- Pull the trigger (hold the trigger to the rear), and the hammer should release.
- Pull the charging handle back, let up on the trigger until you hear the reset, and you should not hear any hammer movement.
- Pull the cocking handle to the rear and return it to its forward position. During the last 1/4" of bolt carrier movement, the hammer should fall.
- Place the weapon on SAFE.

NOTE- If your rifle fails any of these tests, then check your assembly. If the rifle will not pass these checks and it has been assembled properly, contact a qualified gunsmith for assistance.

Inspection and maintenance by the unit armorer- It is essential that the rifle be examined periodically by the armorer, who will check that it is being properly cared for by the user.

All components of the rifle will then be checked for correct functioning. When this examination is made, the following special cleaning and inspection operations will also be carried out:
- Cleaning the exhaust port in the gas cylinder
- Stripping and cleaning the extractor
- Checking the gas setting
- Checking the sight and correcting, if necessary

# Section 3

## Operation and Function

Cycle of Operations (COO) – this starts from a standard reference point: the weapon is loaded, charged, and placed on fire and the trigger is pulled. It will vary based on the type of operating and locking system. Once the operating and locking system is known, the cycle is logical. The cycle of operations is crucial to diagnosing root causes of malfunctions. Each specific malfunction will correspond to a specific step or sometimes two in the COO. A failure in the system at a certain point will by default cause a failure of omission of all subsequent steps (example – a failure to properly extract will manifest as a failure to eject.).

Closed Bolt System– gas operated - Tappet; tilting breech block locking system
- Fire
- Unlock
- Extract
- Eject
- Cock
- Feed
- Chamber
- Lock

**Fire-** Pressing the trigger fires the shot.

**Unlock-** When the bullet passes the gas port in the barrel, part of the combustion gases penetrates the regulator and hence move into the gas cylinder. The piston is driven to the rear and strikes the bolt carrier, which is also driven rearwards. After recoiling a few millimeters, the ramps of the bolt carrier force the rear part of the bolt to rise, thus lifting it out of engagement with its locking shoulder in the receiver. The mechanism is then unlocked.

**Extract-** The recoil of the bolt carrier assembly continues The extractor removes the spent case from the chamber and extraction is completed; then the hammer, pushed by the bolt carrier, is forced to pivot to the rear.

**Eject-** As recoil continues, the base of the spent case contacts the ejector, an integral part of the receiver; the case is then thrown out of the gun to the right through the ejection opening. During this rear movement, the return springs, housed in the butt, are compressed by the bolt carrier rod hinged to the rear of the bolt carrier. The piston has returned to its forward position, as its spring relaxed.

**Cock-** As the bolt carrier assembly travels rearward, it presses the hammer back down into the cocked position and is held by the sear.

**Feed-** The return spring, compressed during the rear movement of the mechanism, now relaxes and drive the bolt carrier assembly forward. The bolt carrier strips from the magazine and pushes the next cartridge towards the chamber.

**Chamber-** The front of the bolt carrier contacts the rear portion of the barrel; the cartridge is chambered and the base of its case seized by the extractor claw.

**Lock-** The bolt carrier acts on the upper shoulder of the bolt carrier and forces its rear end downwards, causing its lock shoulder to engage in the locking recess in the receiver. The mechanism is now locked.

The bolt carrier continues its forward movement alone. Towards the end of its course, the safety sear is tripped by the shoulder on the rear left underside of the bolt carrier, which causes the sear to pivot and the hammer to be released; the rear end of the firing pin protrudes beyond the rear face of the bolt carrier, when the front face of the bolt carrier is fully into battery.

In automatic fire, it is the safety sear which releases the hammer and thus causes the shot to be fired because the trigger sear is not in action in this case, except for the first shot of each burst of fire.

In semi-automatic fire, it is the trigger sear which finally releases the hammer after it has first been released by the safety sear; the mechanism has been so designed that the trigger must be released, then pressed again, to permit the following shot to be fired.

## SELECTOR LEVER

The lever arm can occupy one of the three following positions:
1. An uppermost position "S" SAFE when the rifle is at safe. In this position, if the trigger is pressed, it is impossible to fire because the rounded part of the selector lever arm is over the trigger platform, preventing it from rising to engage the tail of the sear.

2. A rear position "R" REPEAT -- SEMI AUTOMATIC, which sets the mechanism at semi-automatic (single shot); the rear tip of the trigger is now against a shallower bent in the selector lever than in position "A". Pressing the trigger therefore pivots the sear to a lesser degree so that after the first shot has been fired, the hammer will be caught by the sear. This moves slightly forward under the action of its spring and is thus placed in front of the heel of the trigger, i.e., no longer in contact. Firing

another cartridge is therefore impossible if pressure on the trigger is maintained.

3. A front position "A" AUTOMATIC, which sets the mechanism at automatic fire. Before firing, the rear tip of the trigger is now so positioned in relation to the deeper bent in the selector lever axis, that pressing the trigger causes the sear to pivot upwards. The nose of the sear is consequently disengaged from the hammer bent, and firing takes place. In addition, the nose of the trigger sear has been swung downwards so that it cannot contact the hammer, which is controlled by the safety sear only, so long as the trigger is not released. As firing depends on the safety sear, this frees the hammer each time the mechanism closes after the breech is completely locked. Firing is automatic; when the firer releases the trigger, the nose of the sear rises, catches hold of the hammer, which then pushes the sear slightly to the rear; this positions the tail of the sear over the heel of the trigger, and the mechanism is then cocked, ready to fire the next burst.

To continue firing, the trigger must be released; when this is done, the hammer turns slightly under action of its spring. As it is in contact with the sear, it pushes the sear towards the rear so that the tail of the sear comes over the heel of the trigger; pressure on the trigger will now fire the second shot, and so on.

Note: If automatic fire is not required on a military rifle, the selector lever can be removed and another change lever fitted with indent for semi-automatic fire only, i.e. with 2 instead of 3 settings.

## BOLT HOLDING OPEN DEVICE

When the magazine is empty, its follower pushes the holding open device upwards in the pathway of the bolt carrier, which is thus held to the rear, and the firer knows that his magazine is empty. After a filled magazine has been inserted, depress the lever of the holding open device so that the bolt carrier is released and can continue its forward movement.

## Loading the FAL

**NOTE**- Ensure you have 7.62x51mm NATO ammunition. Inspect it for uniformity, cleanliness, and serviceability. Check all cartridges for undented primers and use only issued ammunition.

## Loading the Magazine into an FAL Rifle

## FILLING MAGAZINE

With Magazine Stripper Guide and Stripper Clips

Each rifle is usually supplied with a magazine stripper guide.
- Fit the magazine filler over the mouth of the magazine, with the guides for the loading clip on the side of the magazine rib.
- Insert a loaded clip into the rear guide of the magazine filler.
- With the thumb, as near as possible to the clip, force the rounds down into the magazine.

Without a Magazine Filler

- Use your non-dominant hand to hold the magazine with the front of the magazine toward your fingertips. With your dominant hand, one at a time, place the cartridge over the top of the magazine follower between the feed lips and press the cartridge straight down until it snaps under the feed lips.
- Once the cartridge is under the lip of the magazine body, bolt carrier it fully to the rear so the next round will be allowed to be pushed down.

The magazine can hold 20 cartridges. It is easiest to lay out the number of rounds for each magazine so you don't have to count the rounds as you load the magazine.

Note - After filling a magazine, particularly when a magazine filler has not been used, it is advisable to check the positioning of the cartridges in the magazine by pressing down with the thumb on the last round inserted.

In the event of one or more cartridges not sliding freely inside the magazine (jamming of the point of a round against the front wall), a correct positioning of all the cartridges can be obtained by striking the rear wall or on the bottom of the magazine lightly with the palm of the hand.

## CHARGING AND LOADING

### With an open bolt
- Lock the bolt to the rear with the bolt hold open device.
- Insert a filled magazine, front end foremost, into the magazine well.
- Swing the magazine into position until fully locked. The magazine is then secured at the rear by the magazine catch.
- Press down on the bolt hold open device and hear and see the bolt go fully into battery, thus chambering a round from the magazine.

### With a closed bolt
- Insert a filled magazine, front end foremost, into the magazine well.
- Swing the magazine into position until fully locked. The magazine is then secured at the rear by the magazine catch.
- Take hold of the pistol grip with the right hand. With the left hand, pull the cocking handle (on the left side of the receiver) to the rear and then release it. The forward movement of the bolt carrier will have extracted a cartridge from the magazine and chambered it; locking of the moving parts will have taken place automatically. The rifle is now ready to fire.

**NOTE**: During charging and loading operations, the rifle will be kept at safe (Selector lever set at "S").

## RELOADING

After the last round in the magazine has been fired, the bolt hold open device, operated by the magazine follower, keeps the bolt mechanism to the rear.

- Press the magazine catch.
- Remove the empty magazine by pressing the magazine release and swinging the magazine forward.
- Insert a loaded magazine.
- Charge the rifle by pressing down on the bolt hold open device or pulling the charging handle to the rear and releasing it.

The rifle is now ready to fire again.

## UNLOADING

- Put the rifle on SAFE (selector lever set at "S").
- Remove the magazine by pressing the magazine release and swinging the magazine forward.
- Pull the charging handle fully back to extract and eject the cartridge in the chamber.

- With the charging handle back, press up on the bolt hold open device and release the tension on the charging handle. This will lock the bolt to the rear.
- Inspect the magazine well and chamber to ensure there is no ammunition present.
- Release the cocking handle and let the mechanism go forward.

## GAS REGULATION

Figure 3-1a
Gas completely closed

Figure 3-1b
Gas completely open

The purpose of the gas regulator is to ensure correct functioning of the rifle with maximum gas escape, or, in other words, the minimum intake necessary for normal functioning, without causing undue wear on the various parts of the mechanism.

Turning the gas regulator to the right (clockwise) reduces the opening by which gas escapes, thus increasing the quantity or "intake" gas used to drive the piston to the rear.

Turning the gas regulator to the left (counter-clockwise) causes the opposite effect: gas escape is increased, and the balance available to work the piston is decreased.

By a system of "clicks" and engagement of the gas regulator spring, the regulator has 13 different positions (12 "clicks" to open fully). There will be different configurations of the gas regulator as it will determine which way you turn the adjustments with the orientation of the gas tube. STG58 and L1A1 are opposite so look at the gas port and turn depending on if you need more or less gas to automate the system.

To make setting in any given position easier, figures are engraved on the gas regulator, the figure 1 corresponding to the completely closed position and one figure for every 2 "clicks" opening. Example: When the figure 5 is opposite the gas hole, the gas regulation corresponds to 8 "clicks."

## Method of gas setting

There are several different ways of finding the correct adjustment, but we suggest the following method, which has, we think, proved itself the best:
- Insert an empty magazine in the rifle.
- All firing is carried out by inserting the cartridges by hand, one by one into the empty magazine, through the ejection opening.
- The correct setting is determined by the point at which the holding open device engages the mechanism and holds it to the rear, or fails to do this.

## Regulating the Regulator

Operation 1- Open the gas regulator completely from the gas block, and unscrew by one complete turn so that the figure 7 is in line with the axis of the gas escape hole. This is the fully open position and, when a round is fired, causes a "short recoil," identifiable by the holding open device failing to engage the mechanism.

Operation 2- Close the gas regulator click by click and fire a cartridge after each adjustment until the bolt carrier is held to the rear by the holding open device.

Operation 3- Now verify by firing several cartridges, one after the other, in the way described above.

Operation 4 If any shot results in a failure of the holding open device to engage the mechanism, repeat Operation 3, after closing the gas regulator by one click.

Operation 5 If necessary, repeat Operation 4 until 5 consecutive shots result in the holding open device holding the mechanism to the rear 5 times.

Operation 6 The gas setting for the rifle is now determined, but it is always advisable to allow a small reserve of "working" gas by reducing the gas escape by two additional clicks.

**Figure 3-2a**
**Gas regulator spanner wrench**

**Figure 3-2b**
**Adjusting with a round**

Note - If the special spanner (Figure 3-2a) is not available, adjustment can be made with the point of a cartridge (Figure 3-2b), or even by hand.
Before leaving the factory, every rifle has been adjusted for correct gas setting.

In principle, the shooter should not alter the gas setting; this operation ought to be done in the presence of the unit armorer or an instructor in a perfect world. As the gun gets fouled up with carbon or the piston wears down, adjustments will need to be made by the shooter.

In practice, the force with which the spent cartridge case is ejected gives an invaluable indication of the gas setting. An ejection of cases to 2 meters (6 feet) from the rifle and at a 45-degree angle in relation to the barrel axis can be considered normal. Violent ejection shows that too much gas is being admitted and, in this event, the gas escape must be increased. On the contrary, weak ejection shows that insufficient gas is being taken in and, in this case, the gas escape should be reduced.

## ZEROING

**NOTE**- Different countries and year of manufacture have variations of front and rear sights, so research your rifle for specifics. To adjust a front sight, you move the sight the opposite direction of needed bullet travel change, and on the rear sight, it is in the same direction of the needed bullet travel change.

The rifle is zeroed, i.e., the sights are correctly adjusted, before issued to the user, but it may require some attention to correct for elevation and direction to suit individual needs.

**Figure 3-3a**
200 meter setting

**Figure 3-3b**
600 meter setting

The lowest setting on the rear sight is 200 meters, and that position is all the way to the rear (Figure 3-3a), with increments of 100 meters up to 600 meters (Figure 3-3b).

Such correction must be done by a qualified armorer or an instructor, who will have the special tools to do this.

### Correction for Elevation

Errors in elevation are corrected by screwing the front sight up or down. If it is screwed up, the impact will be moved down and vice-versa. Front sight adjustment is always opposite to the needed change.

A spring detent locates and holds the front sight in position, which forms a clicking device with the 16 equal divisions serrated under the front sight collar; this assists the armorer when calculating movement of the impact. Moving the front sight 1 division (or click) is equal to a variation in impact of 1 cm at 100 meters (approx. 0.39" at 109 yds.).

### Correction for Windage

Errors in windage are corrected by moving the rear sight to the right or left and in the direction the bullet needs to move.

If the impact is to the right of the point sighted, the screw on the left of the sight is loosened and the screw on the right is screwed up, thus moving the sight laterally along its dovetail from right to left. Tighten the screw on the left. When the correction has been made, and before shooting, tighten both screws.

If the impact is to the left of the point sighted, the sight must be moved from left to right.

A movement of 1 division (or click) is equal to a variation in impact (to right or left) of 1 cm at 100 meters (approx. 0.39" at 109 yds.).

## Firing Positions for the FAL Rifle

**Figure 3-4**
**Photo of standing position**

**Figure 3-5**
**Photo of kneeling position**

**Figure 3-6 Photo of prone position**

**Figure 3-7 Supported barricade position**

## Firing the FAL Rifle

    A. Orient downrange or towards the threat.

    B. Push down on the selector lever to the desired rate of fire.

    C. As you orient your sights onto the target, press the trigger straight back so as not to interrupt the sight picture.

    D. When you have completed firing the rifle, place the selector lever into the SAFE (S) position.

## Launching Grenades with the FAL Rifle

The FAL is equipped with a combined device, serving as both flash-hider and grenade-launcher; with this fitment, anti-tank and anti-personnel grenades can be launched with great accuracy.

A special type of ammunition is used, generally known as a propulsive, or grenade cartridge. This cartridge has no bullet, and the mouth of the case is closed by a "star" crimping, which is waxed to ensure complete tightness.

### HANDLING

1. Put the rifle at SAFE.
2. Unload the rifle.
3. Set the rifle for firing single shot.
4. With the left hand, pull the charging handle to the rear and hold it or lock with the bolt hold open device. With the right hand, insert the propulsive cartridge into the chamber. Let the mechanism go forward (it is easier if the muzzle of the gun is held downwards).
5. Put the grenade on the launcher and make sure that it is fully on.
6. Release the safety from the rifle and, as required, remove the grenade safety. The rifle is then ready to fire.

### FIRING POSITIONS

**Direct fire**
For the three usual positions (standing, kneeling, and prone), the method of holding the rifle is the same.

- Grasp the middle of the handguard firmly with the left hand.
- Hold the pistol grip firmly with the right hand, with the index finger securely in front of the trigger.
- Hold the butt under the right armpit, never lean it on the shoulder.

NOTE: A sling can be used to help take the recoil, but this is left to the discretion of the user.

**Indirect fire**
- Dig the heel of the butt into the earth, with the pistol grip up, i.e., towards the firer.
- Incline the rifle at the required angle.
- Hold the foot down on the front of the butt to prevent it from moving out of position.

**NOTE**: As far as possible, it is advisable to avoid positioning the butt against any hard surface, such as concrete, rock, etc. This is particularly important for indirect fire from the prone position, where the shooter naturally tends to anchor the front part of the butt to avoid the effects of recoil.

## FIRING SINGLE SHOT TO LAUNCH A RIFLE GRENADE

- Insert a filled magazine with the grenade launching rounds.
- Use the tip of a cartridge to push the plunger in the gas plug fully down and hold it in this position.
- Turn the cartridge and the gas plug 180 degrees so that the letter "G" appears on top, instead of the letter "A."
- Let the plunger return to its housing (the notch in the plug is towards the bottom).
- Charge the rifle.
- After firing each shot, repeat the charging of the rifle.

## FITTING THE BLANK FIRING DEVICE

This device is to be screwed on the tapped end of the flash hider.

# Section 4

## Performance Problems

### Malfunction and Immediate Action Procedures

Malfunctions are usually preventable through good practices, but they may still occur out of the blue from time to time. Of course, you hope it is on the practice range, but you should treat each one as if you are in a life-or-death situation. Practicing proper and effective corrective actions will allow you to be more confident in your rifle handling. In stressful situations, you can become much more stressed due to an unforeseen malfunction that is easy to correct. I have observed many shooters that perceive themselves to be experienced, but when they encounter a stovepipe, they nearly disassemble the rifle rather than sweep it out and continue.

Malfunction drills must fix the problem 100% of the time (excluding a weapon stoppage — broken weapon) the first time performed. You must look at the rifle and identify the problem (obviously, the rifle is not functioning as you need, so you must transition to another weapon or rectify the situation). It is a non-functioning weapon at this point — fix it.

You should always practice taking a covered position to correct malfunctions with considerations on how you operate.

The following pages in this chapter describe and detail corrective actions for the various malfunctions that may be encountered.

### Stoppages and Immediate Action

The FAL is unlikely to be affected by variations in standard military grade ammunition.

Obviously, this means good quality ammunition because a bad cartridge will give rise to stoppages, whatever the weapon that fires it.

Stoppages are generally of two types:

1. Those caused by fouling, due to the user's negligence, or ignorance of his rifle, or lack of lubrication (modern powders of good quality cause very little fouling).
2. Those caused by some mechanical deficiency (less frequent).

A mechanical stoppage, other than that caused by an empty magazine, can usually be remedied by taking immediate action, without stopping to investigate its cause.

Procedure for immediate action
- Remove the magazine and place it in a pouch or on the ground.
- Pull the cocking handle fully to the rear while looking for a round or casing to be ejected, inspect for a clear chamber, and then release the charging handle.
- Replace the magazine into the magazine well and ensure it is fully locked into position.
- Load (recock the rifle by pulling the cocking handle to the rear and releasing so that a new round is fed into the chamber).
- Resume firing.
- If the stoppage recurs, consult the armorer or instructor to find out the cause.

Made in the USA
Columbia, SC
20 September 2024